ROAR
If You Have To

10 Inspirational
Tales of Success
And The Women
Who Roared

Josefina Bonilla

ISBN (print): 978-1-7344072-0-4
ISBN (e-book): 978-1-7344072-1-1

Published by: RIYHT Media, Inc.

Cover Design by: Yesenia Milan
Interior Design by: Deana Riddle
Editing by: Jan Edwards
Photo Credits: Christopher Huang (image of Josefina Bonilla)

Printed in the United States of America

Dedication

I dedicate this book to all the women—*the doers, the talkers, the relationship builders*—who need a little inspiration and guidance from other women, to stay motivated and connected to their aspirations.

Acknowledgements

I want to acknowledge all of the men and women who have given me a glimmer of hope or an act of kindness and generosity on my path in life, in work, and in the creation of this book.

In particular, I thank my family. Their support in all I have done has been monumental, from purchasing a refrigerator and stocking it full of food when I didn't have money, to taking care of my kids when I had a meeting or event to attend.

I'm so thankful for my sisters of the heart, who have supported and guided me— and kicked my butt more times than I care to admit.

Finally, I am grateful to Russel Pergament, who has been at the forefront of my supporters, as my mentor and my friend. I have truly benefited from his kindness and sage advice.

Foreword

It's been said that if you can see it, you can be it.

That has very much been the case for me during my personal and professional journey, and I know it has also been the case for my dear friend, Josefina Bonilla, during hers.

In this book, Josefina celebrates and pays tribute to the success of "the women who roared", sharing how their success inspired her own, illuminating their individual paths for all to see, and paying it forward to propel the next generation of successful business leaders and entrepreneurs.

In addition to sharing her own inspiring story, Josefina generously shares the stories of ten incredibly amazing women, in their own words, shaped around her ten tenets that will connect with and help keep anyone focused on their own journey of personal and professional growth.

When Josefina asked me to write the foreword for this book, I reflected on how, if it hadn't been for the examples of many extraordinary women who came before me and showed me the way, I would never have been able to accomplish half my ambitions and aspirations.

Like Josefina, I credit the community of exceptional women who coached, advised, mentored, sponsored, or otherwise looked after me along the way, especially those who gave me opportunities that I imagined were beyond my capability at the time, then inspired my confidence by showing me that they believed in me, and ultimately gave me permission to believe in myself. As the saying goes, your candle loses nothing when it lights another.

I hope you enjoy these stories of inspiration as much as I have.

Karen Kaplan
Chairman & CEO, Hill Holliday Group

Contents

Preface

I think that, for years, I've suffered from imposter syndrome, like many women and women of color, though they may not yet realize it, or admit it. When conceptualizing success, I saw other women who resembled what I imagined success to be and what I was not.

For most of my life, my interaction with success had been passive. It was not until I was young and living in California that I wanted to put something in front of me that would not be easy for me to do. I had never been athletic, so I decided to run the Bay to Breakers mini marathon. I trained for weeks and months, running just a little longer, getting just a little better every week until I was ready.

I ran that marathon as if my life depended on it. I wanted to quit so many times; yet I persevered. I cannot express the happiness I felt running through that finish line. I had skated through tests and school and so many other things. That was the first time in my life that I had worked toward and accomplished something so monumental and personally challenging. After that feat, I was sold. It became my new euphoria to set goals and actively achieve them— not through happenstance, and not because it was easy. Success was no longer a passive notion. Success had become, *I can do that, and why wouldn't I?*

Success is a relative and dynamic concept. It's related to where I am in my life at any particular moment and based on whatever achievable goal I have. When either of those changes, my concept of success changes with it. There is an interconnectivity that I can now identify between each goal and everything I do around it. The goal is a living breathing objective.

When I was at State University of New York, Institute of Technology(SUNY), success was about getting my diploma. In working toward a Computer Science degree, I started my first company, AZTech Training, training folks to use computers, because that seemed the most practical thing to do. I was on a mission and had very little time for anything else. My entire life was directly centered around my classes. My circle of friends were professors, clients, and all things SUNY.

The irony of that is that I didn't go to my own graduation. I come from a long line of entrepreneurs and was surrounded by brilliant women, but I was the first in my family to graduate with a Bachelor's degree. Although they saw my degree as important, having my own company was much more impressive to me and my family. I accomplished my two important goals, finishing school and leaving SUNY debt-free.

At the beginning of my career, my focus was on doing and accomplishing. Today, I am less concerned with huge career goals and more aware of others' needs and how I can serve through offering connections and information. Dressing up in accoutrements doesn't resonate for me. I am more about impacting change by helping someone else define their own success.

Increasingly, for me, success is about simplicity—releasing my need for quantity of possessions and accomplishments and replacing those with spiritual and emotional growth. It's a successful day when I can look in the mirror and embrace the belief that I am successful and pay that forward. Recently, someone asked me what elusive gift I would give to my two boys if I could. That gift would be the feeling of working toward something outside of your ability to conceive, and achieving it. *If I could just bottle that...*

"…The true meaning of courage is to be afraid and then—*with your knees knocking and your heart racing*—to step out anyway, even when that step makes sense to nobody but you.

I know that's not easy. But making a bold move is the only way to truly advance toward the grandest vision the universe has for you."

—OPRAH WINFREY

Introduction

A couple of years after creating Color Magazine, I was asked to give a speech in Boston for the Women of ALPFA (Association of Latino Professionals For America). I began writing the speech in the mindset of offering motivation for women to start their own businesses. I wrote the speech as if I were in the audience, to motivate myself, and to hear and receive what I needed to get moving. It was an honest and realistic process that reflected what I had to go through in my journey, the tools I used to get started, and the resources that sustained both my vision and the company.

Women of ALPFA Speech
2009

By Josefina Bonilla

"Hello Everyone! I can't believe that it has been almost two years since I started Color Magazine! I want to share with you my journey as an entrepreneur in the world of publishing.

Some of you might remember, EntreAmigos Magazine. Although EntreAmigos was a product of Hispanic News Press (HNP), I owned a percentage of it, and I handled the content of the publication. HNP handled the business side. I launched EntreAmigos as a way to capture the presence of Latinos at all social, network, and community events. In the middle of the first year, I offered to buy the publication. I wanted to create a publication that was more inclusive and greater than its parts.

Due to a variety of circumstances, I decided to walk away from EntreAmigos. I loved that magazine. It was one of the most difficult things I had to do, but I was on a quest to start my own company and my own magazine. I informed HNP with thirty days notice.

Up to this point, although I had some side personal projects, I'd always had the security of being on salary— and had the lifestyle and shoes to prove it! That month was excruciating. I was afraid. Not only did I have this idea, but I had said it aloud. I had to make it happen. **Lesson #1: Be courageous!**

How was I going to make this happen? I knew how to sell. I knew about content. And I had developed some design skills. I had to quickly figure out all the other things that happen in between and after. So, I shed my close fitting ego, ate a slice of humble pie, and asked a lot of questions. **Lesson #2: Don't be afraid to simply ask!**

I knew I needed a team that I could trust. I had meeting after meeting, developed my first business plan, and recruited people who believed in the idea of my magazine. Running EntreAmigos gave me access to many people. I made a list of those I needed to talk to, some of whom I knew, and some I didn't. I put the naysayers in one corner and the supporters in the other. I got commitments from advertisers, and I put my plan into action. **Lesson #3: Ignore the naysayers.**

There was one name on the list of someone I had wanted to meet for a long time, BostonNow CEO, Russel Pergament. I found out BostonNow was the media sponsor of an event coming up. Hoping to meet him, I attended. I sought out his table, introduced myself, and told him about my idea. He was intrigued, but even more impressed that I had the audacity to approach him in the manner I did. The end result was that Color Magazine débuted as an extended tab in BostonNow in January 2008. **Lesson #4: Be bold!**

Color Magazine quickly gained traction. We had a presence at events. We were meeting people. And the word was out. We had a reputation!

Three months later, BostonNow collapsed, and Color Magazine was homeless. I remember it was on my birthday. I walked into the office, and Russel took me aside to tell me what had transpired that brought our house down. Happy birthday to me. What do you do when in crisis? **Lesson #5: Don't let them see you sweat.**

We met with The Boston Metro, The Boston Globe, and GateHouse Media. They understood the position we were in, but GateHouse was the most welcoming. So, I made a *list of what I expected from them. Let me rephrase that— I made a huge list of what I expected from GateHouse and—to my amazement, they complied. Color Magazine became an insert in a variety of publications, including Brookline Tab, Needham Times, and many others. **Lesson #6: Ask for everything— and expect it!***

*In less than two weeks, we had new offices in the suburbs, a new version of the magazine, and the beginning of endless worry of cash flow. We realized that we had to be back in Boston. After purchasing red drop boxes and navigating the web called City Hall, we were distributing our magazine in both the suburbs and the city and incurring costs faster than we were getting paid. **Lesson #7: Beware of cash flow.***

*When I started Color Magazine, I knew that I also wanted to host an event to honor companies that were committed to inclusion. Thus, The All Inclusive Awards was born. We started promoting the event in September and decided that we needed a good name to give us respectability. After making a list of potential speakers, we determined that Soledad O'Brien was the one we wanted. She represented national appeal, was well recognized, and was a professional woman of Color. The event was in December, so we had just three months to plan, coordinate, and execute. **Lesson #8: Bite off more than you can chew.***

Color Magazine is a year and a half old, and we are constantly facing new challenges and new opportunities, and in the face of adversity, we are— and I am— fearless. Find the courage in yourself to do what you are passionate about. Life is too short to wait on tomorrows. Make it happen today. **Lesson #9: Roar if you have to.**

After I sold Color, as I was approaching the tier end of my contract with GateHouse Media and Color Magazine and preparing for the transition, I was in the process of clearing my office when I found my copy of the speech. Reading it again, it dawned on me that each of my defining experiences formed the threads that would hold the story of Color Magazine together. These threads are the tenets that presented themselves to me, the tenets that I held close as I created Color Magazine.

My realization inspired me to think about my next steps. From that place of inspiration came my desire to write this book and share my experiences with the women who most need to hear them. This book is the story of the leaders who inspired me. It is the story of success, inspiration, belief in oneself, and the tenets that I reconnected with while writing this story.

Chapter 1
Be Courageous

Josefina's Experience

I launched EntreAmigos, a social magazine, as a way to highlight and capture, in images, the changing presence of Latinos in the Greater Boston Area's social, networking, and community events. It seemed that the images presented by most of the area publications completely lacked the inclusion of Latinos.

Although EntreAmigos was a product of Hispanic News Press (HNP,) I owned thirty five percent. My role included managing content, writers, photographers, distribution, advertisers, and traffic, while HNP handled the back end business, including invoices and accounts receivables.

At the end of my first year running EntreAmigos, I offered to either buy the publication or create a new publication in partnership with HNP. I wanted to create a publication whose focus included all ethnic groups in the Greater Boston Area.

Due to a variety of circumstances, I ended up walking away from EntreAmigos, on a quest to start my own company and magazine. The month between my giving notice and leaving was excruciating. I was afraid. I had voiced my idea and dream aloud, so I had to make it happen.

I am proud to say that Color Magazine has reached a decade of being in the forefront of Diversity and Inclusion, creating events and activities, and providing a platform for professionals of color to have a voice. We are are constantly facing new challenges and opportunities, and in the face of adversity, we are— *and I am*— fearless.

I found the courage to do what I was passionate about. Life is too short to wait on tomorrows.

Beverly Edgehill's Experience

I faced a lot of scary, sad, and traumatic moments in my life, and I had the courage to push through them. I was raised in a very tight knit community and felt safe from harm. Right after I graduated from college, I moved away from home and found myself in a very unsupportive relationship. For the first time, I experienced betrayal and began to see the darker side of life. Fortunately, my faith in God brought me through.

The word courageous means: not deterred by danger or pain; undaunted. For me, being courageous is similar to having faith. I live my life on faith, and I encourage others to do the same. When I am afraid, hesitate, or second guess myself, I always come back to having faith. My faith has made me courageous.

Three qualities that made me successful...

Curiosity — I have always been interested in the 'why' that makes a situation what it is. I am intrigued by the relationship between the whole and its parts and am always looking at how one influences the other. For example, for as long as I can remember, I have been interested in knowing how organizational or societal practices influence individuals and how individuals influence organizations and society. This curiosity drives me in my personal and professional life to examine the balance of influence between the two. For example, I've dedicated my career to helping individuals and organizations uncover the personal and systemic impediments to their desired future state. I position myself as standing beside them, examining the factors that facilitate or block their goal achievement. I use my own curiosity to help them see what they may not be able to see because they're 'in it'. To use a reference I've heard before, *I take them up to the balcony* of their situations, and together we look down at the parts to see what might be interfering with the desired outcomes. It's always so rewarding when someone sees what they couldn't see before.

Creativity — I am innovative, in terms of my approach to creating new options for problems and challenges. I love to *think outside the box*. My husband calls me 'The CCO' – *Chief Creative Officer* – for our household. Although the term creativity is typically used to describe artists, I believe we are all creative in one way or another. As I see it, we're creating all the time, so this makes everyone creative. For example, some people are creative in a negative fashion – they focus their attention and resources on destructive forces. Others are creative in a positive manner – they seek to uplift themselves and those around them. The other side of being creative is being resourceful. Creative people are resourceful people. They use ideas, everyday items, people, and circumstances to create new ways to look at and experience problems and/or opportunities. Creative people show the path to creativity as they inspire others to take bold and seemingly out-of-the-ordinary steps to arrive at different outcomes.

Strategic thinker — In addition to being creative, I am a strategic thinker. Being a strategic thinker is more than being able to think outside of the proverbial 'box.' It requires the ability to see the big picture and develop a road map to get to the big picture. The road map includes key milestones and critical stakeholders. Strategic thinking also allows one to make complex ideas and circumstances simple.

A formative experience that put me on my current trajectory...

It's interesting that my formative experience had little to do with my professional aspirations and outcomes. My first marriage provided lessons which have contributed to my being the woman I am today. Through the trials and tribulations of that time, I developed the internal fortitude to persevere and accomplish goals and not let a set back set me back. I learned to believe in my God-given talents and abilities, and I learned that when people don't have your best interest in mind, it's sometimes okay to move on from a relationship with them.

During the period of my first marriage, I recall my mentor asking me a question, *"Have you outgrown the need to suffer?'* This question startled me, because it shined a light on me acting like a victim of the things that were happening around me. She was essentially saying, *things may happen to you – but they don't have to define who you are.* This was the beginning of a lifelong journey of being tuned in to moments when I feel overwhelmed or despondent. When I am in this state, I use the tools at my disposal – *prayer, meditation, the wisdom of my current mentor, and reaching out to friends and family –* to reflect on and determine where I might be suffering and make the necessary changes to be in my life as I choose to be, not as the circumstances are making me feel.

Lessons from my early career that still serve me today...

Some of the lessons from my early career are: *surround yourself with people who represent who and where you want to go; always have a mentor; and look for ways to bring others along.*

There are so many women and men I admire, both people I know personally and those from societal interaction. I look to them for inspiration and study the qualities in them that I desire to cultivate and/or express more of. I believe in the power and benefit of having a mentor. I am well into my career and still have one. Mentors have helped me to see how my behaviors and mental attitudes were undermining me. We all have a blind side. Having a mentor helps me to open my eyes to the things I can't see about myself. Having a mentor also keeps me humble and remembering that there is so much more to life than material things. One of my former mentors said to me, *"Always remember – you are always learning."* I love this, because it sets me up to be in situations where I am doing just that– learning. I am not done, whatever that means. I am still opening and learning and seeing things about me that are great and things that are not so great. The neat thing is that there are everyday situations that I have at my disposal to learn. My current mentor says, *"Your life presents the curriculum you need for the moment."* I find this true all the time!

Naysayer-disbeliever experiences that propelled me forward, instead of backward...

I recall leading an organization that was faced with some operational challenges. I applied the characteristics that describe me–*curiosity, creativity, and strategic thinking*–to create a plan to address the challenges and move the organization forward. It was an extremely challenging time that was made even more challenging, because the people to whom I reported did not support my approach. There was a lot of tension in our relationship, whereas it had been productive prior to my involvement. In my opinion, they were committed to applying a more binary approach to solve the problem, and I was motivated to think outside of the box. In the end, the approach I proposed prevailed, but it took an emotional toll on me and strained our relationship beyond repair. All-in-all, I used the lessons from the experience to propel me forward, not hold me back.

Shedding friends during my journey and growing from the experience...

I subscribe to the idea that people are in our lives for a season and for a reason. Because of this belief, when it's time for me, or others, to move on–*even if it's uncomfortable*–I know it's for a higher good.

I have grown from having people in my life at different times and the lessons I learned from them and the memories we created. Not all changes in my relationships with others were negative or disruptive. It was just time to move on. I've had many relationships with people that were centered around the work we needed to do at the time. They were great companions but when our work was done, our relationship ended. More often than not, it wasn't a formal ending, just less frequent gatherings. For situations that were unproductive, the endings brought relief. Admittedly, though, the full feeling of relief wasn't realized until much after the ending.

Regrets...

The only regret I have is that, very early in my career, I didn't know how to negotiate a salary commensurate with my experience and potential. I recall during my first job out of college, learning from a male colleague that he made $3,000 more than I did. We graduated from the same college and were hired by the same employer to do the same job, but he was making more than I. I knew this wasn't fair, but I didn't know what to do with the information. It wasn't until three jobs later that I took what seemed like a risk at the time and asked for exactly what I thought was an appropriate salary for my value. I was pleasantly surprised that my employer said yes!

Habits, rituals, or practices I use to stay grounded and motivated...

I try my best to create time every morning for prayer and meditation. I take the time to breathe and get quiet and call in the aid of all the higher benevolent beings to help me for the day. I visualize myself calling all the parts of me–*wife, mother, daughter, spiritual seeker, executive*– together in one harmonious whole. I also do a form of Qigong exercise to help me further integrate the meditative state that I begin my morning with. As the day unfolds, I am able to use the memory of my morning experience as a touchstone to bring me back to wholeness.

Three women who inspire me...

Maya Angelou
My former mentor and spiritual teacher
Oprah Winfrey

How i define success...

To me, success is relative, dynamic, and fluid. It is the ability to handle sad moments with grace and dignity and happy moments with unbounded joy. Success is being in a state of openness to learn and love— and also, to suffer and grow. It's being grateful. It's enjoying moments with family and friends throughout your successful life, because you know that connecting with others is what we're here for, not gathering trinkets or external accomplishments. Success is also knowing that, while it is very easy to believe these things, it is equally difficult to live them day-to-day. But, success is not giving up these ideals.

When I look at myself in the mirror...

I see a beautiful woman who is continuing to grow into herself. She is grounded and committed to being used as an instrument for God's will.

Beverly Edgehill Ed.D.
Transformational Leader, Strategic Integrator, Organizational Stabilizer
Boston, Massachusetts

For thirty years, Dr. Beverly Edgehill has been a transformational leader, integrator of large scale change strategies, and a stabilizer for the next stage of organizational change and growth. Dr. Edgehill's roles have been both internal-facing and community-facing, in for-profit and not-for-profit organizations. She is an effective leader, guide, and partner with other leaders in planning and executing transformation strategies.

Dr. Edgehill's particular interest is in the dynamic that occurs at the intersection of organizational activities and individual leadership. As a scholar-practitioner, she is a student of current research and practitioner in assisting leaders with driving institutional performance. Dr. Edgehill embeds emerging frameworks and practices into her approach to leadership and institutional development.

During her tenure as President and CEO of the leadership development organization, The Partnership, Inc., Dr. Edgehill designed revenue-generating talent management and leadership solutions that reflected the changing business priorities of her clients. Through collaboration with the Harvard Business School and academic institution faculties, her legacy leadership development programs have continued to facilitate the graduation of seniors for industry and academia leadership across the United States.

Dr. Edgehill is a former regional selection panelist for the White House Fellows program and completed her studies at Teachers College, Columbia University, with a doctorate in Adult and Organizational Learning. She has taught graduate level courses in leadership, organizational learning, and change management and provides one-to-one mentoring to help career professionals successfully make critical leadership and career transitions. She is a sought after speaker at conferences and workshops and has published several articles on the topic of leadership and organizational change.

Most recently, Dr. Edgehill was recognized as one of Boston's Influential Women by the Women of the Harvard Club and an Unstoppable Woman by the Boston YW. Beverly is married and has two adult children.

Chapter 2
Don't Be Afraid to Simply Ask

Josefina's Experience

My years as an executive at Cargill had taught me how to sell and how to cultivate meaningful partnerships. EntreAmigos had introduced me to the world of content and publishing. I was fortunate to have worked with an exceptional designer at EntreAmigos, Yesenia Milan, who introduced me to the basics of design. She also created all the logos for Color Magazine.

Once I committed myself to starting Color Magazine, I had to make it happen. I had said it aloud and folks had heard me. I quickly had to figure out all the other pieces that needed to happen in between and after.

I shed my snug fitting ego, ate a slice of humble pie, and asked a lot of questions. I sought out experts in the different areas who would be willing to share with me their insights and approaches. I reached out to marketing, social media, and accounting professionals. Not only did I need to know how everything worked; I also had to learn how I could actually make a living doing it!

Alpa Inamdar's Experience

If you are unsure of something, you should always ask for clarity. You must also be open-minded to the response you may get in return. Intelligent questions set the stage for great communication. I sometimes ask questions out of curiosity, or to gain a deeper understanding of a specific topic. I am also not afraid to ask questions that may be considered uncomfortable, because these often lead to very productive conversations.

Three qualities that made me successful...

First, I am a risk-taker. I have learned the importance of taking risks, in order to open up new opportunities. This has helped me advance my career and grow into the person I am today.

Second, I am adaptable to change. Life is constantly changing, so it is extremely important to learn to adjust, even when it is difficult.

Third, I have grit and resilience. These important qualities can get you through the biggest challenges. Life can throw some curveballs at you, but you must keep going despite them. The reward will be that much sweeter in the end.

A formative experience that put me on my current trajectory...

One of my most formative experiences was working for a global engineering firm that contracted for the government. I was tasked with managing a 5 billion dollar nuclear waste cleanup project. It was extremely challenging and so important for my career. It gave me the opportunity to work on a large-scale project where I could expand my leadership abilities and work closely with engineers, environmental specialists, and technologists.

Lessons from my early career that still serve me today...

Very early in my career, I learned that it never helps to be disingenuous. Honesty and owning up to my mistakes have served me well throughout my career. Committing yourself to honesty, helps you grow and become the best version of yourself. Leaders with integrity are not afraid to tell the truth and do the right thing, no matter how difficult. When working with clients, honesty builds that trust that creates a successful relationship.

Naysayer-disbeliever experiences that propelled me forward, instead of backward...

I took a six year hiatus from work after I had my daughter. Most people in the industry told me that it would be very challenging to return to the workforce.

However, this only pushed me to work relentlessly, until I was given an opportunity to work for Goldman Sachs.

Shedding friends during my journey and growing from the experience...

I have shed friends, especially those who first were colleagues and later became the employees I managed. This was very challenging, but I grew from this experience and learned how to balance both friendships and responsibilities.

Regrets...

When I was younger, I had the opportunity to study law and be accepted into a law program. However, I decided to take a lucrative job offer instead. Looking back, I wish I had pursued my Juris Doctor degree, as it would have given me greater perspective and understanding.

Habits, rituals, or practices I use to stay grounded and motivated...

I truly love meditation. Taking the time each day for myself to have peace and calm is so important. It is a great way to feel centered and more focused. Whether I am commuting to work or getting ready for bed, taking this time for myself is truly so valuable.

Three women who inspire me...

Melinda Gates
Michelle Obama
Ruth Bader Ginsburg

How i define success...

Success is setting and accomplishing lofty goals, while simultaneously fostering an environment of collaboration, inclusion, and helping others reach their goals.

When I look at myself in the mirror...

When I look in the mirror, I see someone who has overcome many struggles throughout her career. I see a confident woman who believes in helping other women. I wish I had a female role model who could have helped me when I first entered the industry. Going forward, I hope to help women jumpstart their careers and make well-informed decisions about their futures.

Alpa Inamdar

Head of Americas

BNY Mellon

225 Liberty Street

New York City, NY 10281

Alpa Inamdar is Head of BNY Mellon's Americas Transformation & Program Management Client Implementation, within Client Service Delivery Asset Servicing. Alpa is responsible for the management and oversight of client onboarding and implementations and the oversight of development and execution of cross functional transition plans for new business opportunities and high profile complex initiatives for existing clients. Alpa's team managers are located in Pittsburgh, Boston, and New York. She is also co-chair for BNY Mellon's IMPACT South Asian Leadership Hub and YWCA Partnership Committee, planning and executing client centric and cultural events for all employees of the Bank.

Prior to BNY Mellon, Alpa served as Vice President and Chief of Staff in the Regulatory and Tax Operations Division of Goldman Sachs & Company and global project manager for the Federal Preparedness program. Prior to Goldman Sachs, Alpa was a Cost Allocation Specialist for Societe Generale. She also led various assignments at Fluor Daniel Corporation, including overseeing a $5 billion Nuclear Waste clean-up project and implementing an SAP system. She has a successful track record in risk management, process improvements, and project management.

Alpa is a board member of Pratham and Ascend Pinnacle and has led multiple initiatives to support women in business, including

Women Helping Women in Finance and Take Two. She is a member of the Junior Achievement Program, a Council of Urban Professional, and a United Way Ambassador, as well as a leader of the Next Generation Community Event for the children of Goldman Sachs employees.

Alpa holds a Bachelor of Arts and an MBA in Finance with Cum Laude status from California State University.

Chapter 3
Ignore the Naysayers

Josefina's Experience

Upon informing Hispanic News Press that I was leaving, I knew I had to act quickly and put together a team of people I could trust. After a continual run of meetings, I developed my first business plan and began recruiting people who believed in this idea called Color Magazine.

Running EntreAmigos offered me access to many people, some of whom I knew, and some I didn't. From that base, I made a list of the individuals I needed to talk to, got commitments from advertisers, and put my plan into action.

Through these conversations, I discovered that many folks believed in me, in my capacity to create something, and— *more importantly*— in the mission I had for Color Magazine. It was very clear. I wanted to create a company that would highlight and support our growing community of professionals of Color.

I also discovered that many folks did not like the idea of Color Magazine, or thought me unwise to start my own company. I could barely track the number of potential obstacles they came up with to support their opinions.

Regardless, I was not to be stopped. I made a list of my supporters, and I made a list of the naysayers. From there, I focused my attention and action on the supporters, and I ignored the naysayers. **I knew that if I allowed fear and unsolicited suggestions from others to drive my decision, I would not even get started. I was driven by the simple need to get it done. My constant thought was:** *The worst that could happen is that I never do it.*

Phyllis Barajas's Experience

I went to Omaha South High School, where *"all the Mexican kids go."* I also hung out with the "Anglo" kids. There were a thousand students in my class, and I was a very good student. In spite of that, the counselors never counseled me about college. Talk about naysayers and disbelievers, the prevailing sentiment was, "The Mexican kids–*even the smart ones*–aren't going to make it anyway." For that reason, the counselors chose not to meet with us. One thing that helped me to move past this type of thinking is my family's financial ability to send me to a state college. I enrolled myself. I moved past the disbelievers by not succumbing and by staying focused on my goals and aspirations. I still do this today.

I am a social entrepreneur, a person who establishes an enterprise with the aim of solving social problems or effecting social change. By that definition, I am a change agent. Rarely do others get really excited when I show up. My work and, to some extent, even my youth were about moving beyond the naysayers and the disbelievers. My wish is to change the perception from seeing our community as a deficit to seeing our community as strong, competent, and beautiful in all its diversity. My life's work is dedicated to changing the minds of the naysayers and disbelievers.

Three qualities that made me successful...

Being a Risk taker

Being an Influencer

Being determined, stubborn, and resilient...once I set my mind to something, I just keep going, undeterred.

My grandmother, Felicitas, who I'm named after but never met, said that when my dad complained about the harsh conditions in the fields of Nebraska where he and others worked as migrants, she replied, *"We worked too hard to get this far. We are not going to give up now!"*

My dad never complained to her again. In the end, he did achieve their dreams–*a house, a truck, and his own business!*

A formative experience that put me on my current trajectory...

I was young, married with three young school age children, and had a love of teaching. The Omaha School district, like many others in the 70's, was under scrutiny for their ability to adapt to the growing number of English language learners. It all began in California with Lau v. Nichols, the successful suit brought by a group of Asian families, regarding disparate education. It found that student's civil rights had been violated.

Before that time, I paid little attention to national issues, beyond being an informed individual, though seeds of those values and beliefs had been planted in me. My Dad was a Mexican immigrant and became a successful businessman before I was born. His stories of struggle, survival, resilience, and–*ultimately*–success have stayed with me to this day.

When I was asked to create and implement the first bilingual program in the Omaha Public Schools (OPS), I came face to face with the perception that the dominant culture had of our emergent Mexican/Chicano community. They saw the changes in the composition of the students as a threat to the status quo. I will never forget attending one of the school committee budget hearings. The cost of transportation for the new bilingual program and the OPS football program was juxtaposed, resulting in a decreased budget for sports. In order to pay for the cost of buses to transport the bilingual program students to the program site, there were fewer sports dollars. The implied trade off meant loss of improvements to the district's high school football stadiums. I was naïve and shocked at the building opposition to the resourcing of the new program for English language learners.

Things like that still happen. Today, many will see this as "code" for "anti-immigrant, Hispanic, Latino, Mexican." At times, I am dismayed that we are still having this exchange, but when I see the exceptionally talented Hispanic Latino/Latinx community that participates in our programs, I am encouraged to keep showing up and building new networks of value. Leading that program changed the trajectory of my life forever, creaing an advocate for fairness, equity, and respect.

Lessons from my early career that still serve me today...

From my earlier career, I learned to keep showing up, continue to ask questions, and continue to offer alternatives that will result in a greater sense of shared values and community, as well as the ability to see these shifts in demographics as an opportunity. In addition to the OPS experience that took me and my view of life in a whole new direction, subsequent experiences taught me to be willing to speak up for those who may not be able to do so for themselves.

In the early 1980's, we moved to NYC, where I worked as an adoption social worker for Little Flower Children's

Services. I was the first and only Hispanic Latina in the adoption unit. My job was to place children in adoptive homes. This was gritty, sad, and challenging work. As the social worker assigned to the children in my caseload, I was required to terminate parental rights, usually the mother's. Most of the other adoption social workers in my unit were white, with the exception of one black woman. The children were mostly Black and Hispanic Latino. My background and approach were somewhat different from my colleagues. First, I spoke Spanish, which made it easier for my clients to speak with me about their situation. Second, I understood their feelings of isolation, given the limitations of their understanding of "how things work here." Most of the parents with whom I worked said, *"I'm fighting, because I want my child to know I tried to keep them."* The problem was that most were struggling to keep it together for themselves, let alone for their child. We would talk about what they wanted for their child, to be safe and to have an education— things that most parents want for their children.

I did a couple of things to help them move through this very difficult situation. I engaged them in helping me to plan for their child's future. I promised, and I kept my promise, to write about them in their child's record in a way that would present some of their better qualities. For one mom, I wrote that she loved music and travel and listed her favorite food. For another, I wrote a fond remembrance of her child as a baby. I had the highest rate in our unit of voluntary relinquishments.

I shared with my colleagues some of the life experiences that our clients faced. I also encouraged them to look for placement within the community, rather than taking the children away. I used to tell them, *"You have a white picket fence mentality."* Research suggests that the amount of contact with people of different racial, ethnic, and socioeconomic backgrounds in a work setting has a direct correlation with the percent of placements outside the child's community, race, ethnicity, and background. Little Flower eventually hired a second Hispanic Latina social worker, shortly before I left to move to Boston.

Naysayer-disbeliever experiences that propelled me forward, instead of backward...

I tend to think of naysayer disbeliever situations as opportunities. As my dad used to say, *"Hija, you have to educate the people."* He'd recall that when people responded to him loudly and with some dumb comment (dumb in my young teenage mind), I'd reply, *"He has an accent–he isn't deaf!"*

Fast forward to my Human Resources career in Boston. Diversity was in its infancy in most organizations I was employed with. I was sensitive to the composition of any of the organizations in which I worked, where I–*like many others reading this*–may have been the only, or one of the few Hispanic Latinos in professional and leadership roles. If I made an overt effort to include candidates from diverse backgrounds–*women,*

Hispanic Latino, Black, older, or in need–that entailed my helping to hire managers and the powers that be, which needed extra time. This was when the prevailing mindset was *"Don't fix it if it ain't broke,"* before it was seen as "the right thing to do" or socially responsible. It was hard to make a business case.

In one, though not isolated, instance, I was challenged with my request to get more time to recruit for a position and told, *"We are about quality…"* I was annoyed, and I exaggerated it by feigning shock and replied, *"How does providing a substandard candidate fit with my professional reputation?"* Shocking! Surprising! One can have both quality and diversity. I believe in keeping one's sense of humor, while being an agent of change.

Shedding friends during my journey and growing from the experience…

Sometimes, I think I scare people away. While others just want to focus on the day to day— the challenge of making a living, taking care of their immediate family, spending time with friends— I like to do all those things, but am determined to venture beyond that. I believe in our Hispanic Latino community. I believe that we have what it takes to keep our country great. Now that I have grandchildren, I'm more determined than ever to do what I can to be an influencer, leave the world a little better than when I got here, and– *hopefully*–leave behind others who will continue to move outside their comfort zones and do more than they originally thought they could.

In looking back, there are people who I thought were my friends, but they actually were not. In hindsight, I see that they may have been "using me" or my brand for themselves, and not reciprocating. I still am open to others. I still believe in assuming the best about others, until they demonstrate otherwise. I don't try to get into the other person's head. I am not about figuring out the other person's motive. I assume they will be consistent in their behavior around me and good about championing the shared causes we believe in. But, for those who aren't and don't, life is too short to spend my time and energy around those who are not aligned with me and the things in which I believe.

Regrets...

Neglecting to focus on building wealth is a regret that I share with cohorts. I have learned too late that *"He who has the gold rules."* I have done alright; I own a nice condo; I can spend time doing things with my grandchildren, like going to the Celtics games. But, because I didn't learn about how to build wealth, I wonder how much more I could have done if I had focused on that sooner. What I do know is that, as a consequence, female Latinos are not as financially well off and, therefore, have less influence. I serve on many nonprofit boards and one paid board, boards that make decisions about the direction of the nonprofits. Many times, those nonprofits touch the lives in our Latino community. In a number of instances, I am the only, or one of two Latinos on that board. The discussions and the decisions being made are being made from people with very different perspectives and levels of contact with Latinos. It is so important to build wealth and be in a position to have the time and the access to influence others.

Habits, rituals, or practices I use to stay grounded and motivated...

For most of my adult life, I enjoyed running, working out, biking, hiking, and attending cultural events. Although I still want to do these and entertain friends and have small dinner parties, I'm currently not doing as well in these areas as I have in the past. Getting older means looking at one's mortality. My fifteen-year-old granddaughter Ava entreats me, *"Abuela, you have to live to be really old!"* Her other grandmother has Alzheimer's. I feel a sense of urgency, so I guess that is what motivates me. That is a reminder to me to live each day to its fullest.

Three women who inspire me...

Eleanor Roosevelt – for being a woman ahead of her time, for forging ahead in the face of social norms contrary to forward progress. Her ideas and her thinking on social issues resonates with me.

Delores Marquez, a family friend – for her qualities of decency, loving ways, and sense of fun. Her mother was my mom's Madrina. They were a large Mexican family with whom we spent lots of Sundays when I was a child. I admired her. She was pretty and popular with both the Mexican kids and the Anglo kids. Her Anglo neighbors had invited her on a trip, but she was killed at the age of sixteen in a car accident in Colorado. As a nine-year-old child, I swore that I would live my life in such a way as to honor her. Even now, I think of her and hope that, in some way, I have honored her memory, made contributions to the world that she might have wished to make, and be the leader she might have become.

How i define success…

From the perspective of a social entrepreneur and what keeps me going and pursuing, success is the point at which my life aligns with my inner values. It's creating a more respectful, accepting, and loving world. It's when my life balance shows more wins than losses. It's having loving, caring family and friends. Success is leaving the world a little better, just because I was here. My hope is that those whose lives I've touched will commit to that vision too.

When I look at myself in the mirror...

In general, I like me! I feel blessed with good health. I am proud of the organization I founded. I truly love each and every mentee and mentor who have participated–*admittedly, some more than others*–but they are all examples of what can happen when people build these networks of value, making conexiónes. I am a connector.

I feel blessed that my mind still works reasonably well. I am able to engage with thoughtful, influential people from all backgrounds. They may not agree with me, but they listen. It is always my hope that, over time, we can influence their ability to see us differently, in an increasingly benevolent, and mutually beneficial light.

Phyllis Barajas

CEO, Executive Director

Conexion

75 State Street, 9th Floor

Boston, MA 02109

Social entrepreneur, Phyllis Barajas, is Founder and Chief Executive Officer of *Conexión*, created to develop a pipeline of Hispanic/Latino leaders to equip corporations, nonprofits, and government to effectively address the nation's changing demographics—specifically HispanicLatinos, now the second largest population group in the United States— to benefit the individuals, their organizations, and society as a whole.

In 1994, Phyllis was appointed Deputy Assistant Secretary in the U.S. Department of Education offices of elementary, secondary, and bilingual education by President Clinton. Previously, she served as the first Hispanic-Latino Assistant Dean for Human Resources at Harvard University's Kennedy School of Government. In addition, Phyllis was national Director of Human Resources for Houghton Mifflin Publishing and a core instructor at Boston University School of Management Institute for Nonprofit Management and Leadership.

Phyllis is the first Latina trustee of Eastern Bank since its founding in 1818 and the 2018 inaugural recipient of the Hispanic Heritage Eastern Bank Community Advocacy award.

She is involved with nonprofit boards, including being: trustee of the Beth Israel Deaconess Medical Center; Chair of the BIDMC Community Benefits Committee; on the board of directors of the United Way Boston/Merrimack Valley; trustee of the Boys and Girls Club Boston (BGCB); member of BGCB Trustees Leadership Circle; member of Jobs For the Future; and on the board of directors of Associated Industries of Massachusetts.

Phyllis's awards and recognitions include: 2018 "Inquilinos Boricuas en Acción 50th Anniversary Community Leaders;" one of Boston YWs 2017 "150 Women of Influence;" Girl Scouts of New England 25th Anniversary "Leading Women" Honoree; Comcast Newsmakers/ Massachusetts; Cambridge College President's Advisory Council; and 2016 "Hispanic Lifestyle Latina of Influence." Additional awards and recognitions include: Comcast "Newsmakers Online;" Get Konnected's 8th Anniversary "GK100 Boston's Most Influential People of Color;" 2016 "SBANE Innovations" Award Nominee; El Planeta "Power Meter 100 Most Influential" for five consecutive years; and recipient of 2014 Color Magazine Media Group's Seventh Annual "All Inclusive Awards." Lastly, Phyllis received: the 2013 Get Konnected Boston 5th Anniversary "Leading by Example, Diversity and Inclusion" Award; Boston Business Journal's "20 On the Move" recognition; and The Women of ALPFA

Boston's annual "Excellence in Contribution to the Latino Community" award in 2011.

Phyllis holds a Bachelor of Arts in Education from the University of Nebraska at Omaha and a Master of Arts in Education from Boston University. Phyllis was born and raised in Omaha, Nebraska, the daughter of Mexican immigrants, and currently resides in Boston, Massachusetts.

Chapter 4
Be Bold

Josefina's Experience

On the list of folks that I was determined to meet, one name aroused the most anxiety in me, Russel Pergament. The ultimate publishing entrepreneur, Russel had launched, built, and sold a variety of publications, including AMNewYork, Community Newspapers, and his most recent at the time, BostonNow.

Before I had created the mock of Color Magazine, I had learned that BostonNow was one of the media sponsors of a local event. With the sole intention to meet him, I secured an invitation to attend and arranged for my sister Ana to watch my sons.

On a mission, I arrived, found his table, walked up, and introduced myself to his lovely wife Andi. She introduced me to her husband, and there we stood. Without any trace of awkwardness, I told him about my idea. He was intrigued, but even more impressed that I had the audacity to come up to approach him in the manner I did.

I came to realize that Russel is one of the most generous people on the planet, but I did not know that then. I had to overcome my fear of meeting an icon and move with boldness and certainty toward my goal. As a result, Color Magazine débuted in BostonNow as a pull out insert in January of 2008.

Amelia Ceja's Experience

A **bold** person is confident, fearless, and courageous and has the ability to take risks. I possess all those qualities. It takes a lot of guts to launch a winery, because there's no turning back, and the competition is fierce. I knew I had to be bold enough to trust and follow my instincts, because I understood the wine industry from every angle, and I was prepared to succeed.

Three qualities that made me successful...

Patience — the wine industry is a long term investment.

Innovation — there's much competition in the wine industry. Finding ways to stay ahead of the curve and predict trends is imperative.

Tenacity — I never give up.

A formative experience that put me on my current trajectory...

I was a young Mexican immigrant girl when I arrived in Napa Valley in 1967. I did not speak English when I started working in the vineyards on weekends. When I told my dad that I was going to have a vineyard of my own someday, he replied, *"Yes you will mijita."* Now, my family and I own some of the most respected vineyards in both Napa and Sonoma, and we launched our Ceja Vineyards brand in 2001.

Lessons from my early career that still serve me today...

Due to demographic changes, the wine industry is continually evolving. Innovation is key. Our company has always remained nimble and adapting to new available technologies.

Naysayer-disbeliever experiences that propelled me forward, instead of backward...

When Ceja Vineyards was launched, the wine industry's focus was only in promoting wine paired with Northern European/Mediterranean food. I love world cuisine, especially Mexican food, and I began preparing authentic Mexican menus and pairing them with our delicious Ceja wines. Everyone thought I was crazy and ridiculed me, but I proved how lovely Mexican cuisine tastes when paired with balanced wine.

Shedding friends during my journey and growing from the experience...

I've always been fortunate to be surrounded with friends who like me and respect me, just the way I am.

Regrets...

Family partnerships are wonderful, but also challenging. I wish we'd established a better job description for all the partners.

Habits, rituals, or practices I use to stay grounded and motivated...

Daily exercise and cooking are my favorite therapies to help me stay healthy and motivated, while exploring flavor profiles in food that pair well with wine.

Three women who inspire me...

Mamá Chepa — my maternal grandmother, a great cook and our village matriarch. She was kind, loving, and generous, and she inspired me to pursue interests outside of my comfort zone.

Frida Kahlo — talented and 20th century's most recognized iconic Renaissance woman, despite suffering many health and gender setbacks.

Alexandria Ocasio-Cortez — politician and activist. I have great admiration for her for doing a fantastic job as the U.S. Representative for New York's 14th congressional district. She's young, and I look forward to witnessing her bright and admirable future.

How i define success...

Success is the positive achievement of my business and personal goals. Success is not just about money or power, nor the growth of my company Ceja Vineyards. It's liking myself. It's having a loving relationship with my family and friends. It's finding ways to contribute to the welfare of my community. Success is a way of life.

When I look at myself in the mirror...

I see a woman who's gone from vineyard worker to award winning vintner in one of the most competitive and difficult to penetrate industries. The wine industry is dominated by northern European males, with few women, and even fewer women of color in power. As president of Ceja Vineyards, I'm in a position to help change the present and future of how wine is sold in this country, by making wine exploration more democratic. There's no need to know anything about wine to enjoy it!

Amelia Ceja Morán
President & CEO
Ceja Vineyards
1016 Las Amigas Rd
Napa, CA 94559

Amelia Morán Ceja was born in Las Flores, Jalisco, Mexico, where she learned the value of ingredients grown organically and prepared with care at the side of her grandmother, Mamá Chepa. She migrated to the United States in 1967 to join her father, Felipe Morán, a farmworker in Rutherford, Napa Valley. On her first weekend in the States, Amelia was in the vineyard harvesting grapes alongside her family at Robert Mondavi's famed Tokalon Vineyard. It was there that she met her future husband, Pedro Ceja. Amelia fell in love with grape growing, and throughout her teenage and college years, she continued working in the vineyards during school vacations to gain deeper understanding about viticulture and winemaking.

Her vision of a career in food and wine became clear while studying history and literature at UC San Diego, as she created authentic Mexican dinners paired with wine for her friends. In 1980, Amelia and Pedro were married. In 1983, Amelia, Pedro, his brother Armando, and his parents, Pablo and Juanita, purchased their first property in Carneros, Napa Valley. They planted their first grapes in the Carneros AVA in 1986. Amelia, Pedro, Armando, and his wife Martha founded Ceja Vineyards in 1999, and today, the family owns 115 acres in the Napa and Sonoma Valleys.

Amelia has become an impassioned advocate for the value and fair treatment of farm workers, following in the footsteps of her father's work with Cesar Chavez and the United Farm Workers labor union in the early 1970s. In 2016, Amelia received the Dolores Huerta Farmworker Justice Award for her successful advocacy for Worker Protection Standard on pesticides.

Her leadership as President and CEO of Ceja Vineyards is groundbreaking, as she became the first Mexican-American woman ever to be elected president of a winery in 1999. In 2005, the California Legislature recognized Amelia as "Woman of the Year" for "breaking the glass ceiling in a very competitive business."

Ceja Vineyards produces 7,000 cases per year, with Armando serving as winemaker. Amelia launched video blogs in 2008 on preparing Mexican cuisine and pairing it with wine, embracing both her Mexican heritage and American home. Amelia combines the best of what she finds in food and drink, tradition and innovation. Her family's dedication to environmentally conscious business practices, sustainable agriculture, and gentle handling of the grapes in the cellar can be tasted in every sip of their legendary estate grown wines.

Chapter 5
Don't Let Them See You Sweat

Josefina's Experience

Part of the agreement I made with Russel included office space in the BostonNow Headquarters for my team and me and the printing and distribution of Color Magazine within the BostonNow publication.

Three months after I started Color Magazine and after we had moved into their offices, BostonNow shut down operations. Iceland was BostonNow's major investor, and their economy was collapsing.

I remember walking into our offices and Russel taking me aside to tell me what had transpired to bring our house down. It was my birthday. I was in shock, but there was no time to waste. I took my team out to lunch and explained to them what had happened. Then, I gave them the day off and declared that we would resume operations the next morning— *at my house.*

What do you do when a crisis hits? You carve out another way. For one month, my team and I worked out of my house and coffee shops before moving into our new offices in Needham, MA.

Lisa Coleman's Experience

The thing about negotiation is that it can seem daunting at times. We have to de-stigmatize the term and all that is associated with it. The thing to remember is that we negotiate all kinds of things every day. We negotiate for our children, our health, the traffic, and other areas of life. We do this for our well-being and for those we love and care about. So, for our collective well-being and equity, we have to advocate practically, asking for what we need and deserve. Negotiation is about remaining calm and thinking things through, just like we do in other daily needs.

As an individual, I work on this every day. I think some do this more than others. In our jobs sometimes— *particularly for women, people of color, lgbtq+, and first generation folks*— it might seem as though we are asking for too much. The wife of a friend of mine says that she wants the "white man with children deal." This may sound like I'm identifying a particular race and/ or gender, but what I mean is this: I want to negotiate the best deal. Historically, there are groups who have received opportunities that others have not. This is what I always ask for in every new opportunity, access to those opportunities. What I've realized is that we can negotiate salary, housing, childcare, vacations, job locations, healthcare, and so much more. Negotiating is key in many of our life experiences.

Three qualities that made me successful...

Three qualities that have made me successful are: my being a learner; my curiosity; and my serving with joy. I have often defined myself as a servant leader. In other words, I work on behalf of others, promoting and creating innovative possibilities that have not existed before. I try to bring a great deal of laughter and joy to this work. This is vital when we're working in partnership with others and in-service to others. Being curious and a constant learner has been crucial to creating innovation and entrepreneurial spaces, both within and outside of traditional organizational structures.

A formative experience that put me on my current trajectory...

Two experiences that probably shaped my life the most were working with homeless populations and working with people in hospitals (in the Buddy system) during the early years of the HIV crisis. In both cases, what I was struck by was the humanity of people— volunteers, medical staff, and others who worked tirelessly to help those in need. I was also struck by the inhumanity of some who refused to recognize the humanity of others, out of self-protection or lack of compassion. These experiences were invaluable lessons as I began to do my life's work.

Lessons from my early career that still serve me today...

The lessons that serve me best from my early career taught me to be courageous, build my posse, and be humble. It's important to be courageous, even when it's sometimes hard, or not popular. It's important to build really strong support systems— both inside and outside of work. And it's always important to approach one's work with a sense of humility, no matter how successful one becomes.

Naysayer-disbeliever experiences that propelled me forward, instead of backward...

When I was in school, and early in my career, I did not receive the kind of encouragement that you might assume, given that I have five degrees now. Initially, naysayers told me that I would probably not complete college. After I completed my third master's degree and enrolled in my PhD program at one of the top universities in the country, I sure thought those naysayers were wrong. The key is to not let someone else's expectations of you predict what will happen in the present or future.

Shedding friends during my journey and growing from the experience...

Yes, I've had to move on from some friends. I wish them well on their journeys. I think we all have different journeys. Sometimes, those journeys grow apart. I think—*or hope*—that I've learned how to be compassionate and not disregard others or get rid of them, and just understand that we have different journeys. I have also gotten better at knowing what I need for support and how to create a mutually supportive posse. It's not a one-way street in any way.

Regrets...

I have no regrets, only lessons.

Habits, rituals, or practices I use to stay grounded and motivated...

I try to take good care of myself, although I'm not very good at it sometimes. It ebbs and flows. Yoga, meditation, and self care are important to me, and I need to get better at developing a regular practice of them. I also love to garden. I love to cook. And I love to be with my friends and other loved ones, to laugh, have a good time, and be joyful.

Three women who inspire me...

There are so many women who have contributed in all types of ways to my formation. Instead of trying to choose just three, what I can say is that the women who inspire me are women who have broken the rules, women who have forged ahead in the face of adversity, and women who have gone about their work and their lives with great joy. I think joy is key to doing good work. These are the qualities of all of the women I would list.

How i define success…

Success is not something I think about that much. I think about learning, about service, about living a joyful life, and about creating loving spaces. I guess that is success to me.

When I look at myself in the mirror…

I see someone who is trying to do her best and continues to do so. I see someone who hopes that she has helped as many as she could along the way and someone who has been helped by so many along her way. I see the generations of women before me and what they poured into me from birth until today. I see a woman who hopes she's doing them all proud.

Lisa Coleman, Ph.D.
Senior Vice President Global Inclusion and Strategic Innovation
New York University
70 Washington Square South
New York, New York 10012

Dr. Lisa M. Coleman is New York University's (NYU) inaugural Senior VP of Global Inclusion and Strategic Innovation. Reporting to the President, Dr. Coleman works with senior leaders, internal stakeholders, external partners, and constituents. Her team is responsible for the advancement, promotion, and capacity building for strategic global inclusion, diversity, equity, belonging, and innovation initiatives across NYU. This global reach includes New York, Shanghai, Abu Dhabi, NYU's other thirteen sites, and numerous global centers.

Prior to NYU, Dr. Coleman served as the first Chief Diversity Officer and Special Assistant to the President at Harvard University from 2010 to 2017, where she and her team developed some of the first initiatives focused on the intersections of technology and disability. Prior to NYU and Harvard, she directed the Africana program at Tufts University and was later appointed to serve as that institution's first Senior Inclusion Executive, reporting to the president.

Dr. Coleman's scholarly work was sparked by her early professional and research work with the Association of American Medical Colleges, Merrill Lynch Inc., and as an independent computer consultant for various for-profit organizations. Dr. Coleman has spent over twenty years working with numerous colleges

61

and universities and for-profit and nonprofit organizations, on leadership, global inclusion and diversity, innovation, and technology.

Dr. Coleman continues to advise and consult with C-suite leaders globally, and her current work focuses on the global inter- and transdisciplinary intersections of innovation and inclusion within and across cultures. She sits on various national and international boards and is the recipient of numerous awards, recognitions, and honors of excellence in teaching, leadership, and her work on global diversity, inclusion, belonging, equity, and innovation.

Dr. Coleman earned her doctorate from NYU in Social and Cultural Analysis, American Studies and three Master of Science degrees from Ohio State University in: African and African American Studies; Women's, Gender, and Sexuality Studies; and Communication Studies.

Chapter 6
Ask for Everything...and Expect It!

Josefina's Experience

In a mere three months, Color Magazine had traction. We were representing our publication at events. We were meeting people. And the word was out. We had developed a reputation! Now, we needed to find a home.

Thanks to Russel's credit and leadership, we were introduced to other publication leaders, including The Boston Metro, The Boston Globe, and GateHouse Media. They understood the position we were in, a publication without a home.

Color Magazine became an insert in a variety of publications, from Brookline Tab to Needham Times and many others. Of all the publications, GateHouse was the most welcoming. During my final meeting with them, I made a list of things that we needed. Let me rephrase that. I made a huge list of things we needed. To my amazement, they said *"Yes."*

Kip Hollister's Experience

After opening up the staffing company at age twenty-six, my business partner backed out on me. I had no idea what it meant to run a company, lead a company, or fund a company. But, I did it anyway. In my mind, if I failed, I'd still be able to get up the next day and be okay. I had this vision that I could do it, and I decided to. I knew what I wanted, focused on the vision, and expected it to manifest.

When we clear away our fears and tap into our desires, we truly are able to manifest the life of our dreams. Now, this does not mean that there is no work involved. But, if we can stay in the present moment of what we want, come from a place of expecting that it can be accomplished, and then take right action steps forward, the rest takes care of itself. We must simply stay out of our heads and patterns of limiting beliefs and live from our hearts' desires!

Three qualities that made me successful...

One quality that made me successful is accepting that I don't know what I don't know, and doing it anyway.

Another is humility. I find that I'm always very coachable. I don't need to be the one who knows all the answers. And I don't like it to be all about me. I like it to be about others.

The third is listening to the naysayers, rather than ignoring them. I want to listen, because they may have some good points and views. I then tune inward and look at what I am choosing to do and make a conscious choice for what's right for me.

A formative experience that put me on my current trajectory...

Oh, my gosh, there were so many. One was really learning to have humility, being able to be transparent and vulnerable. I used my vulnerability to put really good people around me who I could also learn from and around whom I didn't need to have all the masks on, pretending that I knew what I was doing. It worked to my benefit, though I didn't know this at the time. I gained a lot more credibility and trust. I build credibility and trust. I think that being a leader takes being vulnerable and humble, so others truly believe you and follow you.

We had some really tough times in the beginning. I hit a recession. It was being fearless through the recession, being a transparent communicator with my colleagues, letting them know exactly what was going on, and letting them know that we were going to have to work a little bit harder, but we would make it that enabled us to come out the other side of it. So, it was working through my own fears—and their fears—to build a cohesive team of trust and collaboration, because it's not about one person. It's about a team.

It's about building it, especially in the infant years of growing a company. It's not one person who can make the firm happen and grow. The leader has to know how to pull other people in and create that collaboration.

Lessons from my early career that still serve me today...

Listening is critical—listening to what others have to say and listening to other people's viewpoints and opinions.

What has served me is not needing to be right. I don't ever feel that I need to be right, and that's still serves me today.

Taking risks. If I'm not out of my comfort zone on a daily basis, I'm not leading.

Naysayer-disbeliever experiences that propelled me forward, instead of backward...

With the birth of the Hollister Institute, I had more naysayers and disbelievers than I'd ever had in my life. Back in 2015, I'd build a big meditation room, which no one could ever believe I would do at 75 State Street. They thought I was crazy. I was off my rocker.

To open the institute was against a lot of people's viewpoints about what the business world needed. But I trusted my intuition. I relied on my intuition and my own self worth, to be determined to make it happen.

Shedding friends during my journey and growing from the experience...

I think there are people who come in and out of your life to help you get to where you are, and then you outgrow them, or they outgrow you— one of the other. I am always wanting to do, learn, and grow, but some people aren't interested in that. And that's okay.

I think that growing from that experience means not holding any ill will toward another human being, but accepting that our paths are going in two different directions. We're on different journeys. I've accepted that, surrendered to it, and embraced it.

Regrets...

I have many regrets, one of which is that I lead the company for twelve years without reaching outside to get coaching and support. I had the imposter syndrome going, which believes that if I reach out, they're going to find out that I'm not worthy and not good enough, but the exact opposite happens.

Another regret is, as a leader in my younger years, I cared a little bit too much about being popular with my staff, rather than making some good, hard, tough decisions that would have served the well-being for all.

Habits, rituals, or practices I use to stay grounded and motivated...

Before bed, I write in my journal of gratitude and appreciation. I usually go to sleep each night with a meditation tape. What we focus on when we go to sleep is what marinates in our minds for those hours, so it's critical to be clear of stress, worry, and anger. If we're not free of that, it's helpful to choose a meditation tape that can soothe us.

When I wake up, I write in my journal of gratitude and appreciation and then meditate for ten to twenty minutes. I follow that up by writing any observations I had during the meditation and set my intentions for the day.

Afterward, on at least three mornings each week, I work out, even if only for a half hour. I gave up judging myself for small workouts. Short workouts are better than no workouts.

Then, I drink a cup of warm water with lemon and ginger, followed a short while later with vitamins and a smoothie for a nutritious start.

I listen to Abraham Hicks religiously on my ride into work, to align my energy. To stay grounded, in addition to my journaling and meditation, I focus on living my future now, meaning that I pay no attention to what is not and only focus on what I want to happen, as if it has already happened. I choose deliberate and conscious thinking that aligns with feeling good, not bad. That means, no negative self talk, no complaints about how things are not. If I feel anxious, I tap on my meridian points. Deep breathing grounds me throughout the day.

Three women who inspire me...

Grace Andrews — one of my personal coaches and a coach for my organization

Maya Angelo — who I absolutely love and adore

Michele Obama — who I really respect

How I define success...

I am successful when I tune inward, listen to my inner soul speak, and hear what it is that makes me shine with delight, joy, and a sense of wonder. When I am tuned into this space, I can create.

When I look at myself in the mirror...

Over the years, I've done a lot of work around looking in that mirror, not loving who I saw, and now I'm able to look in the mirror and love who I am. I feel as if I will continue this work. I feel as if I'm on this life journey to continue to love myself, nurture myself, and grow myself, so that I can be the best I can be, for myself and other people. I now know that the more I give to myself and accept who I am, the greater gift I will be to humanity.

Kip Hollister
Founder and CEO
Hollister Staffing
75 State Street, 9th Floor
Boston, MA 02109

Kip Hollister created Hollister Staffing in 1988 and has developed it into one of New England's premier woman-owned recruiting firms. Kip attributes Hollister's success to the trust and integrity of its leadership. Her passion, as Founder and CEO, to create a thriving business culture led to the 2015 launch of Hollister Institute, which supports individuals and teams through customizing unified and energized work environments designed to enhance productivity.

In addition to offering mindfulness workshops for high school students, Kip has developed a number of programs at the Institute, such as: Communication and Conflict Resolution; Managing Stress Through Mindfulness; Networking and Your Personal Brand; Mindfulness in the Workplace; The Art of Feedback; and a series of leadership courses focused on helping leaders inspire and nurture a growth environment for themselves and their teams. As a certified leadership coach, Kip's aim couples leadership development and management training with executive coaching.

Kip has served on numerous boards, including: The Workforce Investment Board; The Workforce Development Committee of

Massachusetts; Advisory Boards of the YMCA Training Inc.; Cristo Rey; Everybody Wins; and the Alliance for Business Leaders. She currently sits on the boards of The Commonwealth Institute, a non-profit organization devoted to advancing businesswomen in leadership positions, and Recovery Works, an organization dedicated to combating the stigma associated with substance abuse by helping recovering addicts re-enter the workforce.

Kip's passion, commitment, and leadership in the Boston community has raised the bar for community and corporate social responsibility. She is a 2012 Ernst & Young Entrepreneur of the Year Award winner and national finalist. Kip lives in Dover, Massachusetts with her husband and their four children.

Chapter 7
Make It Easy for Others to Say Yes to You

Josefina's Experience

In order for us to continue running Color Magazine, we had to find advertisers and supporters. I focused all my efforts on helping people say *"Yes"* to us. As a matter of fact, that focus still helps me today. Folks want to be part of something they believe in, and our part of that is helping them to see how they fit into a greater good. Color Magazine is all about that.

For example, when composing an email message, rather than using the phrase, *"My previous email contained pertinent information…,"* provide all the information in that email, so that the individual doesn't have to leave that email to refer to another place and time to retrieve the rest of the information, in order to make a decision. Everything needed is right there in that current email.

From the collateral material to the printed magazine and email communications, we focused on making sure the recipients had everything they needed to easily say *"Yes."*

Yao Huang's Experience

When you're doing deals on a regular basis, most of what needs to happen is to persuade the other side to say yes. You do this through compromise, reading people, patience, and finding win-wins, so that everyone is aligned. I have spent a lot of time reading, to learn how to do that.

Three qualities that made me successful...

Grit is something I've had to use through many difficult experiences. It's been a very long road. I've been on the entrepreneurial side of building companies and in the dirt with all the founders. It takes a lot to make it through the ups and the downs. It's easy to be successful when there are lots of money and resources. It's harder when you are trying to jumpstart something from scratch, or when there are not enough resources and manpower, and you have to push things through. Occasionally, things don't always go your way, or people are against you. Yet, despite the challenges, you're still going and find it in yourself to still do what needs to be done.

Confidence was taught to me through my parents' giving me the belief that I could do anything. At the beginning of the tech phase, we realized that no one else knew anything either. A lot of what we were building was being built for the first time. Being in enough meetings where my confidence was able to push opportunities through really showed me that having a good team fueled that confidence. Having the knowledge, being ready, being prepared, and knowing that we would do anything to make sure our goals were achieved really fueled this overwhelming feeling that I could do anything, because I was surrounded by fantastic people.

Humor is something I've learned more recently. People obviously like to work with those they like and those who have a sense of humor. I've implemented it on public stages, gatherings, meals, and meetings, and it's really just about relaxing and not taking everything so seriously. And with that comes this shedding of the stress and pressure to always be the best— and the decision to just enjoy life and the people around you. Humor is a good way to see who someone really is and if you can have fun together. Life's too short. I need to work with people I enjoy. We actually need to have some fun sometimes.

A formative experience that put me on my current trajectory...

I wanted to be a Renaissance person. It's kind of like what old masters used to do. They would learn and read and study almost everything, to be a painter, astronomer, or something. I didn't believe that going to school to learn one thing determined that the rest of my life would be that one thing. I thought I could do everything I wanted to do. I wanted to excel in sports, business, and medicine. I thought I could do it all.

I thought, *Why not start with the hardest thing*—science, medicine, and chemistry. So, I went to school for pharmacy. Later I switched to technology. Then I'd gotten my series seven, to do investment banking. After that, I went into investing. Eventually, I tried standup comedy.

I want to try everything in this life, and I believe I can be anything and do anything. It takes practice. It takes will. It takes interest. I kind of look at life through what it presents and through my changing interests, drive, and direction. I think it's this mindset of what makes me happy and what I enjoy that's directing each of the next steps. That's something I don't think a lot of people understand. I don't have a twenty year plan, or even a five year plan as to what's going to happen next. I feel, I know, I seek, and I assess each of the next sets of opportunities one at a time, with a core basis that guides my decisions. It is by happiness, not a degree or financial security, that I'm driven. It's based purely on joy.

Lessons from my early career that still serve me today...

The lessons that still serve me are learning how to make fast friends and how to quickly capture attention, present, persuade, and sell. These things were not taught in school. I had an amazing boss and mentor who talked with me and impressed on me what leadership could look like and how to develop those people skills.

Without good people around you, you're not really able to rally them and persuade them that anything is possible. You have to do work with others who are better at certain things than you are. You have to work with your team. These skills that I learned early had never been taught anywhere else. They were good examples that truly strengthened me over the years.

Naysayer-disbeliever experiences that propelled me forward, instead of backward...

Most people are pessimistic, so dealing with people who have never done it before, or people who don't think they can do it themselves is an ongoing journey that happens every day, even now. I've decided more recently not to share all my ideas with everyone but just do them. I block out negativity. I've blocked people from my life who are negative; they don't really add value.

I listen to criticism if it's helpful. Good criticism comes from someone having experienced something similar and advising where not to step and what options are available. It takes a lot more words and time and advice and caring than to simply say something is not possible because it's never been done. One of the reasons I hear this so much is that I'm often venturing into projects, production, companies, and initiatives that are newly created. It's fun finding ways around existing systems to see how we can push something new through. I am propelled forward every day by the things that I do and what they can accomplish for the larger masses.

shedding friends during my journey and growing from the experience...

I've absolutely shed friends, including one of my best friends. I think that we all change and move apart. Building companies and managing people who are responsible for other's futures made me grow up fast. Sometimes people grow apart and change. You cannot stay thirteen or twenty one forever. It's not about clubbing anymore. My needs and friendships have changed as I've gotten older. I've needed people to be more present, more wise, better advisors, more dependable, less frivolous. It doesn't mean that you can't have fun; it just means that I need more out of friendships, and I found that through maturity. I've also learned a lot about human nature, greed, how people's love of money drives decisions, and the makeup of a person. Friendship is not developed with just anyone.

Regrets...

I have no regrets, but a huge lesson learned. When something is not working, or it's dead, chop it all fast. It's natural to have a bond, but the ability to let go fast saves a lot of time and money. That is a lesson that I would share.

I think the makeup of our lives helps us grow and learn, learn about people and learn about how to make decisions— without which, I would never get to each of the next steps and be where I am today.

Habits, rituals, or practices I use to stay grounded and motivated...

I get shocked responses from this all the time. I don't drink coffee or alcohol. I wake up to a happy music playlist that gets me bopping to start my day with this positive flow of energy. I listen to a lot of comedy. I want to laugh every day. I don't take things too seriously. I always lead with my rabbit's foot. I visit my mom as much as I can, which reminds me where I come from and not to take things for granted. If you want to stay grounded, fly coach. That will get you motivated really quickly to get your knees out of the back of the chairs in front of you and maybe lie down one day.

I only work on game-changing projects, and being a part of that change motivates me to keep going, to find purpose, to leave a mark— and not to merely exist, but always to build something new. I really enjoyed helping the underdogs, like the Wonder Woman dinner series, helping women bond authentically and as a group. I close gaps by speaking to board and senior positions. That's what keeps me going.

Three women who inspire me...

Oprah—because you have to, for the amazing things she does and because she continues to challenge herself and do more and more and more.

Tiffany haddish—for her refreshing cherry display of humor in life, despite the fact that her life was hard. She's damn funny and just cracks me up. I love her glow of positivity.

My mother—for what she slaved through to get my sister and me to become who we are. She built a business and a life out of nothing. I find it amazing that she did that as an immigrant who didn't speak English and was held under the traditions of housewife responsibilities. She's finally getting to relax.

How i define success…

Success is commonly defined by money or titles. As such, this association only pushes the determination upon society, or your "tiger mom," and enables you to take the easy way out, without thinking about what you want and what makes you happy— *which is different for everyone.* What I want and what makes me happy is freedom— the ability to make decisions and do what I want each day, whether that is to take a month long trip to Capetown, build a spa, or invest in and open opportunities for women in film. These don't all go together and definitely zig zag a bit, but that's how success works. It is the ability to have ideas and make them a reality. Turning them into reality requires a level of freedom of time and place and the ability to pull resources and teams together to execute. It turns out that there is a basic structure involved in creating. Creating something once triggers our emotional and mental ability to do it again. All of this requires experience and a life-long journey of doing and accomplishing. Success takes time, but it is time well-spent and worth every lesson, connection, and accomplishment.

When I look at myself in the mirror...

I see that I've got a lot more to do. I'm super excited about the future, because the resources I have available now are more abundant than when I started. The person I've become is one who embraces the silliness of who I am and is comfortable enough to laugh loudly and be who I am, where the younger version had split them into two people— one for the nine to five and the other for the five to nine.

Yao Huang

Founder

The Hatchery

123 William St, Floor 19

New York, NY 10038

Yao is Founder and Managing Partner of The Hatchery, an organization that has been instrumental in developing the New York technology ecosystem. Hatchery's big data incubator works with corporations to collaboratively develop new innovations and companies, for competitive advantage and revenue streams, leveraging machine learning, artificial intelligence, prediction, and natural language processing. She has helped over 350 early stage companies through various phases of maturity, with a focus on product, business, revenue, and funding. She leads the enterprise incubator in New York, building products with corporate partners, from ideation, development, sales, and funding, to exit. She is advisor and deal maker to the governments of ten countries throughout North America, Europe, and Asia, assisting foreign technology companies in their expansion to the U.S. market.

Yao was named one of eleven women at the center of New York's digital scene by *Forbes*, one of 25 Women Driving New York's Tech Scene by *Beta Beat*, and one of the 100 Most Influential People in Tech by *TechWeek*. She is part of the U.S. State Department Global Entrepreneurship Program Delegations, bringing entrepreneurship and initiatives to strategic countries.

Yao is a sought after speaker in the areas of internet company building, technology, innovation, and entrepreneurship. Yao and her efforts have been featured in: *Fortune; Inc Magazine; The Miami Herald; Reuters; Daily News; Red Herring; Crains; American Venture;* and *TED*. She has a particular passion for helping entrepreneurs, women, and social causes with projects focused on building global communities and pushing more women into executive positions.

Chapter 8
Beware of Cash Flow

Josefina's Experience

In less than two weeks, Color Magazine had new offices and a new insert version of the magazine that fit into GateHouse Media's publications. After purchasing red drop boxes and navigating the web known as City Hall, we were distributing Color Magazine via GateHouse, in both the suburbs and the city and incurring costs faster than we were paid. And so began the endless worry of cash flow.

A big part of being successful in media advertising and publication is insuring your ability to run operations, pay your employees, and take the actions you need to take in order to grow your business. This requires a thorough understanding of how and when advertisers pay for their ad space, which was not something we could regularly control. I came to the conclusion fairly quickly that we needed to create additional sources of revenue.

Diana Lee's Experience

After I had my baby, I really didn't want a full time position where I had to work a nine to six every single day. I really wanted fun and flexibility, so I formed an LLC. My clients were auto manufacturers— Volkswagen, BMW, Ford Motor Company. Some had dealerships that were going under, in trouble financially. My job was to do a full financial audit of what happened and then— from the perspective of an outsider— give them a consulting plan to turn it around. The common themes I noticed were around cash flow situations. A lot of these were debt-like, and realizing that cash flow was somehow diminishing, based on lack of cash flow. They had gone too far and they weren't collecting things on time.

One of the things I always did was work on getting receivables, because receivables will immediately tell you whether you're able to collect or not. The older the receivables got, the lower the chances were that they would be able to collect, especially anything after ninety days. I was looking at thirty, sixty, and ninety day receivables. My talks with these dealerships involved telling them that if they're not collecting the money and they really don't have a full strong collection plan, each day that goes by after thirty days has less chance of ever collecting that money.

So, that experience is something we knew when we launched Constellation Agency. I didn't let bills go past thirty days. I had teams of people reaching out to collect that money. If you don't do this you'll easily go to sixty, and then you'll easily go to ninety days. As customers realize that you're not going to take them down, they're going to be a lot more lax, knowing you're not one of the vendors that they have to pay. They'll pay vendors that are not lax.

I could not be CEO and also collect, so I had to immediately put a team in place to do that type of collection. We have layers of collection. It's funny, because we are a strong collection department. I've had clients say that we're like the Mafia. It's true. It's what you have to do. You need to have courage, and you also need to believe that you deserve that money. It's really up to you to say, *"I am owed that money, and you deserve to give it to me."* If not, they're going to be lax. Not once have I ever had a cancellation. Never. Because people said, *"Oh, I don't like your collection policy,"* and *"We like the fact that you respect yourself enough to collect that money."* It's having courage and knowing that that money is yours.

Three qualities that made me successful...

Passion. Belief in myself. Self-love.

Have you ever watched the video *Dream Crazier*? It's the new Nike commercial they just filmed with women. I love that commercial, but when I saw that it was of women athletes running, I realized that they were basically saying, *Women who ran a marathon were called crazy. Women are crazy if they yell and cry.*

Yes, we've got to be passionate about things, but if we want to be the best at our game, we need to do more than sacrifice, work hard, and be determined. The number one thing we have to do before we can do all of that is love ourselves.

When I first started Constellation, I was in my car for nine hours a day, driving from one client to the next. Pitching. Doors closed. A lot of the men said, *"Yeah, not good enough. Because the concept, Diana, you know. When you actually have something better, you can come back."* Nobody wanted to be the first one to try anything. Nobody believed in me. Everybody was a naysayer. If I didn't believe in myself, I wouldn't get back in that car and drive another nine-hour day from site to site to keep pitching. If I didn't believe in myself, I would have given up.

There's a lot of negativity out there. So many people say you can't do it, or you won't be able to, and it's because of that that you won't be able to. If you don't have that self-love to push through all that, you are not gonna do it. That's where you have to start. The passion has to come from the self-love, from the belief in yourself.

A formative experience that put me on my current trajectory...

My parents came out of the Korean War wanting to find a better life for their families. So we immigrated here back in the seventies when I was five years old, and we didn't have anything. I mean, we were really, really poor. My parents had to work fifteen hours a day every single day. By five in the morning, they were already at work. So, at the age of six and five, my sister and I had to take care of ourselves. We had to walk to school by ourselves, come home by ourselves, feed ourselves, dress ourselves, and get ourselves in and out of bed.

My dad loved all of us so very much and was committed to making sure that our family survived during those times. He worried about me. What I mean by that is that I was the only Asian child who couldn't do math well. He is an engineer and really smart, and he would say, *"I can't understand why you are doing badly in math."* He would tell my mom, sister, and family members all the time that they were going to have to take care of me for the rest of my life because I couldn't do math and I wasn't very smart. From a very young age, my sister was told to promise that she would fend for me when she grew up, because I wasn't going to be able to fend for myself. I heard this and, though I knew it came from a place of love, in my mind, I was saying, *I will show him— I'm going to be successful, and no matter what, I'm going to be driven.* And that thought drove me.

You have to believe in yourself right from the get-go. Nobody else can do it for you. You've got to do it for yourself. It's your choice. That's why I always talk about self love. Nobody else can give self-love to you. My parents loved me, but in their mindset, they really viewed this as a handicap that was going to affect me for the rest of my life. If I didn't do that for myself, I would have believed them.

Lessons from my early career that still serve me today...

One of the lessons I learned, and one that still serves me, is risk taking— *a lot of risk taking*— like believing in myself enough to take a risk. But I wouldn't have been able to do it without advocates around me. I was doing fine financially and really well in my consulting company and working with a manufacturer. I didn't need to launch Constellation and have all these people in the company to support. I could have kept doing what I was doing.

It was my husband who said, *"No, Diana. You always say to me and everybody else that you would have done it differently if it were your company. You would not do it this way. You always criticize the company that you're with and say, 'If they just listened to me and did it this way, it would be more profitable. It would be better.' So you're almost going to be fifty. When are you gonna do it? At this point, if you don't do it now, you're never going to do it. You're secure enough that you can do it. And I'm here to support you, to make sure that you live the dream that you want to live. So, either you take the risk now, or you are never, ever going to do it. So don't keep talking about it."*

And that was it. Those were the words that created the momentum I needed. It was my husband helping me through that. It was having an advocate— *and a male advocate*— because male advocates can be so important. If you have strong male advocates with you, allowing you to take a risk and believing in you, you can be a powerhouse. If you're going to be an entrepreneur, you need to actually understand risk and take risks, especially if you want to be successful.

Naysayer-disbeliever experiences that propelled me forward, instead of backward...

I am in a male dominated industry. 90% of my clients are in the automotive industry— BMW of America, Jaguar, Land Rover. Less than 17% of people in the automotive retail industry are women. There are only a few certified digital providers for all the automotive manufacturers. There are around twenty who support all the manufacturers in the U.S. We are one of those twenty. The other nineteen are men. There are naysayers all around me.

Shedding friends during my journey and growing from the experience...

I have a core group of girlfriends I've known since elementary and highschool, and they will always be my core group of friends. I do think that as you get more successful in life, and as you create more wealth in your life— *I hate to say this, but*— there are a lot of people who come out and ask you for things. Your clients, your friends, your this person, that person, and that other person. And at the beginning, you are trying to help them. Then, you realize that there are just too many of them, and every one of them is asking for a favor. You can only help a certain amount of people, right? So, you do the best that you can. Sometimes, there are more people asking you for that extra favor, so you really need to pick and choose, in terms of what is going to be the most beneficial and important to you. Eventually, you end up isolating yourself more, because it's happening more frequently than ever before.

People ask if I ever resent it. I really don't. A therapist told me a long time ago, *"When you give, give your whole heart, without having any expectations. Otherwise, don't give it."*

Regrets...

I have a lot of regrets. I think some are because I was female, and I was Asian, and I was in the automotive industry. Early on, I was really tough— *not that I'm not tough now*— but I felt I had to prove myself and my worth to people by being extra tough. I was dealing with a lot of men, especially during the first ten years of my career when I was in retail management. Being a twenty five year old Asian woman, managing forty-five- to fifty-year-old men meant I needed to prove that I was the manager and that they needed to listen to me.

I was either hit on, or talked down to. They'd say very inappropriate things to me a lot of times. Because of that, I was extra guarded, extra tough, and tried extra hard to prove to myself and to them that I was higher than they were. I never socialized with them or did anything fun with them, because I thought that was a place for them to abuse me in some way. That's a regret of mine. Now that my inside matches my outside, and I know myself, I'm not trying to prove to anyone that I belong here. I needed that maturity, which took a while to figure out.

Habits, rituals, or practices I use to stay grounded and motivated...

Being close to my family and spending time with them in our home on the weekends keeps me grounded. Being close to my spouse and having weekly dinner dates with him helps me process the difficulties of my league. He has been my therapist through my most difficult workplace experiences. Having a close relationship with my family members has kept me sane.

Three women who inspire me…

Katherine Lee—my daughter, inspires me, because I want more for her future. I don't want her to go through all of the trials that I had to experience being in business in male-dominated industries. I worry about that. The things I've seen, witnessed, and heard haven't always been appropriate and have, in many ways, been demeaning toward both women and humanity. I don't want her to have that same set of experiences.

Liz Elting—Forbes contributor, Founder of Elizabeth Elting Foundation, and former CEO of TransPerfect Translations, inspires me, because I see her as very calm during a storm. She has weathered a lot of pain and business hardships; yet she is so positive, kind, and supportive, even— and especially— during the worst of times. You never really see Liz Elting have a bad day.

Arianna Huffington—author, business woman, creator of Huffington Post and Thrive Global inspires me. She revealed that she is a workaholic, which I identify with. She described how she had worked so many hours in a row that she passed out at her desk, cutting her face, and was rushed to the hospital. As a result, she realized that, no matter how much work was there in front of her, she would never be able to complete it in one day, and she needed to find work/life balance. I resonate with this, because I haven't found work/life balance. I think her mission is a great reminder for all of us to take care of ourselves first. She started a new company to educate companies on work wellness balance. That's a great step for us all.

How i define success…

If I knew what success was, I think I would have already stopped. My quest to find success pushes me to achieve more every day.

When I look at myself in the mirror...

I think that, in many ways, I'm one of the most self-critical people. Good or bad, it's one of the things that pushes me to do better. I don't think a lot of women like looking in the mirror, and I count myself among them.

Diana Lee

Co-Founder and CEO

Constellation Agency

110 William Street

New York, New York 10038

"If you don't jump, you're never going to do it." These were the words of encouragement that moved Diana Lee, ELI-MP to leverage her thirty years of automotive experience to launch Constellation Agency in 2016, a digital advertising and marketing technology

company.   Diana oversees the operations, sales, and client relations aspects at Constellation. She also prioritizes Diversity and Inclusion in each aspect of the company, from its executive team and staff to its commitment to multicultural, in-language digital marketing products.

Since its founding to 2017, Constellation has reported around 700% revenue growth. While Constellation's future looks bright, rapid growth in such a short period of time presents its own challenges. From starting the company without any office space to moving six times in two years and hiring talented candidates to meet increasing client demand, Diana continually pivoted and adapted. Having become a successful certified digital media provider for the Volkswagen Digital Dealer Program and supporter of numerous Audi dealers in the Northeast, Lee was more than equipped to rise to the challenge.

While pursuing her coaching degree, she learned that being a leader involves asking more questions and that the answers we need can be found within us. Lee is driven by a belief that growth comes with faith in yourself and a willingness to take risks. Lee empowers the women of Constellation Agency to challenge the status quo of the male-dominated automotive industry and coaches her team to *"be the wolf, not little red riding hood"* and *"not to feel bad for asking for what you deserve."* She is proud to represent multicultural communities as a leader in diverse marketing and believes that supporting and advocating for each other is the only way to make the world a better place for the next generation.

Chapter 9
Bite Off More Than You Can Chew

Josefina's Experience

In addition to creating advertising revenue for Color Magazine, I also created the All Inclusive Awards (AIA), an annual December event honoring companies committed to Inclusion. We began promoting the event in September and decided that we needed a high profile and respected speaker to attract attention and attendance. After making a list of potential speakers, we determined that Soledad O'Brien was a woman who represented national appeal, was well recognized, and was a professional of Color. She was the one we needed. We had three months to plan, coordinate, and execute. It was a monumental task, but we pulled it off.

The AIA was Color's first event. When we saw a market need, we added the Women of Color Leadership Conference, The Men of Color Leadership Conference, and others. There were times when we worked on several events simultaneously and had to chunk up the day, in terms of which event to focus on during that chunk. It was the only way to get everything done without getting stressed and overwhelmed. I had actually learned that skill from raising my boys who had ADHD. I had to chunk up the information they needed to receive and understand, so that they wouldn't be overstimulated and fail to process.

What I learned is that you have to be ready to take on all that you intend. By being strategic with your plans, you can handle more than you think you can, though you can't always know or guarantee the cadence of your success.

Yvonne Garcia's Experience

I have always taken on great challenges in my academic and professional journeys. Often times, I wonder how I'm going to get through it. But in the end, I succeed. It comes with great sacrifice and determination, but in the end, I get it done, and I feel great pride.

Three qualities that made me successful...

Empathy—my ability to understand that all individuals are fighting battles we know nothing about— is a reminder to be kind always.

Leadership—I always look to take on roles in which I can drive change and leave all that I led in a better place.

Passion—giving my all to anything I commit to and leading with my heart and mind make me an authentic leader.

A formative experience that put me on my current trajectory...

Taking an assignment in China to launch a private bank in Beijing certainly shaped my career. It opened doors for global opportunities and allowed me to gain a global perspective throughout the rest of my career.

Lessons from my early career that still serve me today...

Being a broker at Merrill Lynch taught me how to problem solve. It was critical to understand both my clients' desired end state and their current situation, in order to help them achieve their short and long term goals. The ability to design a blueprint that will achieve my future goals, by realizing specific milestones throughout my personal and professional journey, is a practice I have leveraged throughout my entire career.

Naysayer-disbeliever experiences that propelled me forward, instead of backward...

I always say that if you don't have naysayers, you are doing something wrong. Naysayers are usually attracted to individuals who are driving change, creating impact, and moving things forward. Throughout the earlier years of my career, as a result of not reacting to the actions of a few naysayers, I enjoyed many promotions and new opportunities.

Shedding friends during my journey and growing from the experience...

At times, life presents you with a different path and different opportunities. Sometimes, your friends join you on the journey, and sometimes, they stay behind. I have always focused on the road ahead and welcome my friends to join me on the journey.

Regrets...

I wish I had slowed down and appreciated the lessons each opportunity presented. I remember doing my MBA full time, while having a newborn at home, and working full time as a broker. I never got to appreciate each experience in its individuality and totality.

Habits, rituals, or practices I use to stay grounded and motivated...

I run marathons, because they challenge my mind and body and remind me how strong I am. I enjoy spending time with my kids, who remind me of the great responsibility I have to raise individuals with high integrity and a strong work ethic, so that they may contribute positively to society.

Three women who inspire me...

My mother—for her integrity, work ethic, and commitment to family

My daughter—for her leadership, perseverance, and passion for all that she does

My sister—for her empathy and ability to focus on what matters most in life

How i define success...

Success means living my true purpose and impacting the lives of others, by inspiring them to do more than what they thought was within their reach. Success for me would be my legacy of making a difference in the world by acting with urgency in what matters most in our lives. Success is serving as a role model for our youth, working hard to transform corporate America, and opening the doors to those who do not yet have a seat at the table.

When I look at myself in the mirror...

I see a strong woman who has benefited from the guidance of many wonderful accomplished individuals from all circles of life. I see a woman who has worked hard to achieve great things, but still has a long road ahead.

Yvonne Garcia
Chief of Staff
1 Lincoln St
Boston, MA 02111

Yvonne Garcia serves as Chief of Staff to State Street's CEO, Ron O'Hanley. Yvonne was named one of the top 50 Most Powerful Latinas in the US in 2017 and 2018 by *Fortune Magazine,* and *Latino Leaders Magazine* named her one of the nation's Top 12 Leaders in Finance in 2016 and one of the nation's Top 5 Latina Executives in 2012. *The Boston Business Journal* named Yvonne one of 2015's Top 22 Most Influential Women in Massachusetts, and she received the NFL Hispanic Leadership Award from the New England Patriots in 2018.

Earlier in her career, Yvonne served as Director of Marketing and Distribution Strategy for Liberty Mutual, leading development and deployment of complex integrated marketing strategies, including their Hispanic Marketing initiative and Liberty Mutual's segmentation strategy for Personal Markets. Additionally, Yvonne served as Vice President of Mass Affluent Marketing for Bank of America. In her role of Vice President for their China Construction Bank Strategic Assistance Program, Yvonne and her team created and implemented over five new Wealth Management Centers throughout China, resulting in over eighty centers throughout the country currently.

An active leader of local and national communities, Yvonne serves as chairwoman for ALPFA, the largest Latino professional organization in the country. She also serves as Chair of the Hispanic Scholarship Fund for Boston and for the Board of Directors for The Partnership, Inc. Additionally, Yvonne is the co-founding Chair of Milagros Para Niños, a board at Children's Hospital in Boston, which has raised more than $8.2 million in funds for Hispanic children who can't afford medical care. Yvonne was appointed by Massachusetts Governor Charlie Baker to serve on the state's Latino Advisory Commission Board and was most recently appointed Chairwoman for the Greater Boston Chamber's Women's Network Advisory Board.

Yvonne is a fully certified Six Sigma Black Belt and has run nine marathons in the past seven years and applies that discipline, rigor, and process to every project she deploys. Yvonne holds an MBA from Boston University in Finance and Marketing and a Bachelor of Arts degree from SUNY Albany. She is a graduate of the ARMY R.O.T.C. program at Siena College in Loudonville, NY and holds a Certificate in Economics and Culture from La Sorbonne in Paris, France. Most recently, Yvonne was awarded an honorary degree in Doctor of Humane Letters from Cambridge College in Boston, Massachusetts.

Chapter 10
Roar If You Have To

Josefina's Experience

After the initial success of Color Magazine, I attended an event for professionals of color hosted by a large media outlet in Boston and brought the first edition of Color with me. I was proud, so proud.

Color's president at that time walked over to me and asked me why I had not talked to them before launching Color. *"I had, in fact, spoken to you first, when it was simply an idea,"* I replied, *"and you passed on it."*

Immediately after the president walked away, The media outlet's publisher, one of the most influential people in Boston at the time, came up to me. He looked around the room, pasted a smile on his face, looked at me, and said, *"I am going to crush you like a bug."*

Everything went to slow motion. As I watched the people slowly walking around the room, his smile turned into a sneer. I wanted to run like a cowardly lion out of the room. Instead, I put a smile on my face and responded, *"Just because we are in a little competition does not mean we can't be friends. And, I don't scare off that easily."*

When I left the event, I was furious. I swore under my breath with each step back to my car. *How dare he!?* As I shut my car door, I opened my mouth and let out a roar so loud that I looked around to see if anyone had heard me. All the frustration, all the fear, and all the emotion I had been holding back, I let go in that expression. There was absolutely no way that I was going to let him intimidate me.

My head hurt. My throat burned. But I felt empowered. Then I laughed out loud at myself.

Kamil Ali-Jackson's Experience

Roar frequently and–*when necessary*–roar literally. When you are a black female professional in corporate America, everyone is ready to give you plenty to do, make you do it in as short a time as possible and with as few resources as possible, expect you to "do the impossible" each and every time, and then take credit for your accomplishments— especially "your impossible feat." Therefore, you have to let them know *at "Hello"* that you do not suffer fools lightly, you take no prisoners, and you will take all the credit you have earned and that is due to you.

Three qualities that made me successful...

Passion for life—I intentionally did not say work. My passion for life is what keeps me going.

Ability to see the miracles—I see miracles in the ordinary, everywhere, and in everything I do. This makes life very interesting, *and never boring*.

Inexhaustible Energy—I never rest. If there is anything left to be done before morning comes, I do it.

A formative experience that put me on my current trajectory...

I strongly disagreed with my black female supervisor about a particular legal position on a project that I was handling. She ended up telling me that if I did not follow her instructions, I would be disciplined, including termination. I did not follow her instructions. I called my three sisters, my husband, and my father–*in that order*. I vented for hours on the telephone with my family members, repeating over and over again the rightness of my position and–*in my opinion*–the wrongness of her position. Then I immediately started looking for another job.

I found a better one with a strong black male who valued excellence. He only hired people he felt comfortable delegating responsibility to. He had a very high opinion of his own skills and, therefore, had high expectations for the people who worked for him. He understood that power is built from the ground up. If you hire good people, it will only make you look smarter and more talented.

Because of that "push," I left a big pharmaceutical company and ended up founding several small pharmaceutical companies and creating jobs, not only for myself, but for many others. I thought the big pharmaceutical company was the "gold standard." Ultimately, I discovered that was not the case. I am forever grateful to the supervisor who threatened to fire me for not following her directions. If not for that, I would never have left.

Lessons from my early career that still serve me today...

Hire well. I look for people who are talented and highly skilled. I believe that if you hire excellence, you will receive excellence. Hire people who have their own internal benchmark of high standards that motivates them to give their best, and they will give you their best, all day long, every day.

Finish now. I always finish today, never leave it for tomorrow. This gives me a head start over others who believe that tomorrow will come. Because of the death of my first born and only son, at the age of three, I know that tomorrow may not come.

Fear nothing. Your job is a job. It is not your life. You can fail at your job and still succeed at life. Don't be afraid to fail. My husband's favorite saying by Winston Churchill is, *"Success is never final, and failure is never fatal."* If failure is not fatal, what are you afraid of? As my mother used to say, *"This too shall pass."* Because the worst happened to me–*the death of my only son*–I keep another saying close to heart: *"Fear not the future, the worst has happened to me."*

Get up. I get up every morning. That is an accomplishment that should not be underestimated.

Naysayer-disbeliever experiences that propelled me forward, instead of backward...

In my performance evaluation at a prior job with a law firm, I was ranked lower than I thought I should have been, compared to other fifth year associates. When I saw my ranking, I immediately started looking for another job. I went on to become an international transactional attorney, traveling all over the world. I also became a General Counsel and Chief Legal Officer of several small pharmaceutical companies and, eventually, a serial entrepreneur. Again, I thank the supervisor who underestimated me. He reminded me that no one defines how good I am, but me. So, I jumped, *and I never looked back.*

As a result of that experience, I tell young lawyers not to listen to other people's characterization of their skills. If you know you can write, stick with your self-assessment and move on. Try to learn as much as you can from each person you work for, but don't let them define you, your skills, your abilities, or your possibilities.

Shedding friends during my journey and growing from the experience...

I lost friends, as part of my life journey, *not my career journey*. In 1994, my firstborn and only son, Ross, died in a car accident. I was the driver. After that experience, without consciously realizing it, I started to focus only on my work and my family. As a result of living my life looking inward, I forgot to nurture my friendships. And I lost them.

It took decades for me to come back to myself. My mother, Ruth, my toddler daughter, Kendall, my husband, Michael, my three sisters, Sharon, Karen, and Cheryl, and my brother, Patrick each, in their own way, provided me with the lifelines I needed at that time to get up in the morning. Ultimately, I realized that no one was going to pick me up off the floor. If I stayed lying on the floor, I would be stepped on, *or stepped over*. So, I got up. I haven't sat down since.

Regrets...

I have many regrets, like forgetting to nurture my friendships. Once I started looking outward again,

I decided to try to help everyone I met, someway, somehow. If they asked me for help, I tried to do as much as possible for them. I'm sorry if I was not there for my friends along the way, but now I try to "pay it forward." A young Indian woman told me that her father told her to always go through life with her hands stretched outward, with her palms open to the other person. This lets favors flow out to others and from others in to you. If you keep your hands in the shape of fists, nothing flows out, but nothing can flow in either. It is now my life's mission to help the historically and currently disadvantaged.

I regret not jumping out of corporate America earlier in my career. Now I say, *"Take the risk!"* This does not mean quit your job. It means, make plans and take action while you have the youth, energy, opportunities, and money.

I regret that my mother, Ruth, is not here to see that I survived, and that I'm thriving, even with Ross in my thoughts every day.

Habits, rituals, or practices I use to stay grounded and motivated...

I get up every morning. Any obstacle that I face in life and work is nothing compared to having to take my three-year-old son off of life support. The battles I have engaged in and endured have only empowered me and made me stronger and more committed to helping the historically and currently disadvantaged. So, I get up every morning.

I walk firmly, I talk loudly, and I laugh out loud, all the time. At work, they hear me coming down the hallway.

I look at pictures of babies. Who can be angry or sad when looking at a picture of a baby? A baby is a pure bundle of possibilities. I can only imagine good things are going to happen when I look at pictures of babies.

Three women who inspire me...

I have four women who inspire me.

Ruth Ali—my mother, who suffered from bipolar disease and died from kidney failure, as a result of her life-long use of a drug that controlled her mental illness. As a result of her mental illness, the environment in which she lived, and her life choices, she never lived up to her potential. But she was always up, never sad, never depressed. That is the Ali way. If she could be happy with what little she had, how could I, *with all of my opportunities and advantages*, be sad? My mother showed me that happiness is a matter of perspective, and only your perspective matters. She used to say, *"Nothing beats a failure but a try."*

Sharon Ali—my oldest sister, who is entering a new career phase at age sixty-four. She is the head of a medical marijuana company. She has always been "the first" in our family–*the first to attend college, the first class of women at Dartmouth College, the first double Ivy League graduate in our family, the first and only member of our family to get an MBA, and the first to get a job in corporate America.* She is a great role model for each of her sisters who came after her and each of her nieces and nephews. She did more than survive in corporate America— *she thrived.* She has taken the best of what she learned there to use in her own company.

Karen Ali—my second oldest sister, who never met a stranger. She helps anyone who asks–*and those who don't ask.* She goes above and beyond to provide the gift of her time, advice, and resources. At sixty-two, Karen has high expectations for anyone who works with her, because she has high expectations for herself. She only asks of you what she is also willing to give. Karen was never athletic, but when she went to Princeton, she joined the women's track team and ended up setting a college record in hurdles. Karen is a role model for, *"Nothing beats a failure but a try."*

Cheryl Ali—my youngest sister, whose life took an unexpected turn in her fifty-eighth year, when she became a mother without a husband. She raised her daughter, Brittany, to become a very accomplished young woman and attorney. After her husband, Dan, suffered a stroke, she became the mother, father, and 24-hour supporter for her other two children, Madison and Dylan. As a working mother, she always put her children first and gave as much time and effort to them as she did to her work. She is a great example of getting priorities straight–family first; everything and everyone else second.

How i define success...

Success is not having it all. That is greed. Success is creating jobs, not only for myself, but also for others. Success is using my hiring and purchasing power to establish, promote, and implement Diversity and Inclusion initiatives inside and outside of my company. If I feed myself, I'm the only one who survives. It's a lonely existence. If I give other disadvantaged people the opportunity to earn a living, so that they can feed themselves and their families, an entire community, of which I can be a part of, survives and thrives.

When I look at myself in the mirror...

I see a sixty-year-old mother of four, Ross, Kendall, Karis, and Kamryn, passionate about life. Nothing and no one is going to bring me down, *or keep me down.* Maya Angelou was right. I *still rise.* But I also strive to help others rise with me.

Because of my three sisters, I am frozen in time. I am, and will always be, in the same pecking order–the third sister and second to the youngest. For me, that is a good thing, because my position in life never changes. As a result, I am as passionate about life and its possibilities as I was when I was an eighteen-year-old college freshman.

Kamil Ali-Jackson

Chief Legal Officer, Chief Compliance Officer, Corporate Secretary

Aclaris Therapeutics Inc.

640 Lee Road Suite 200

Wayne, PA 19087

Kamil Ali-Jackson, Esq. co-founded Aclaris Therapeutics Inc. in 2012 and has served as Chief Legal Officer since its inception. With more than thirty years of experience in the legal and pharmaceutical industries, Kamil is also the Chief Compliance Officer and Corporate Secretary of Aclaris.

Since 2011, Kamil has also served as the Chief Legal Officer of NeXeption and its affiliates. From 2014 to 2015, Kamil was the Chief Legal Officer of Ralexar Therapeutics Inc. (formerly known as Alexar Therapeutics Inc.). Previously, Kamil served as a legal counsel and a licensing business executive for a number of pharmaceutical companies, including Merck & Co. Inc., Dr. Reddy's Laboratories Ltd., and Endo Pharmaceuticals Inc.

Kamil received her Juris Doctorate from Harvard Law School and her Bachelor of Arts degree in politics from Princeton University. She was a 2011 Philadelphia Business Journal Women of Distinction winner and a 2015 Pepper Hamilton, LLP Remarkable Alumna. Kamil has served on several nonprofit boards and is currently on the board of Rosemont College, a private liberal arts college located in Pennsylvania.

Today

After selling Color Magazine to GateHouse Media, I stayed on to shepherd it through the acquisition. On a daily basis, for almost three years, I used one or more of the ten tenets.

After deciding to write and title this book "Roar If You Have To," during the writing process, I abbreviated it to its acronym, RIYHT. After having written that for the umteenth time one day, I looked at RIYHT (pronounced "RIGHT") and thought, *What a great name for a new company.* That day, RIYHT Media was conceived. As I segued from shepherding Color Magazine into developing RIYHT Media, the ten tenets were what fortified me and kept me focused.

The core of RIYHT Media is based on social responsibility of corporations, creating value for both the corporation's brand and its community. As such, I am planning a RIYHT event and magazine centered around corporate social responsibility. My passion for Diversity and Inclusion is woven through my new company and everything I do in both my work and my life.

I am so incredibly grateful to have found inspiration and learned so much from the great leaders quoted in this book and many more. Success is not happenstance. It takes time and effort. We have to be deliberate in knowing the things we want and the life we want to live, including the ways in which we interact with the many varieties of people around us. I like the whole idea that each of us can choose what works for us, selecting that which best serves us. The tenets in this book have served me well and continue to be an integral part of my life.

"Here's to strong women.
May we know them.
May we be them.
May we raise them."

~ Anonymous

be courageous

don't be afraid to simply ask

ignore the naysayers

be bold

don't let them see you sweat

ask for everything— and expect it

make it easy for others to say yes

beware of cash flow

bite off more than you can chew

roar if you have to

About Josefina Bonilla

Josefina Bonilla is the CEO of RIYHT (Roar If You Have To) Media. Launched in October 2018, RIYHT Media creates value for brand and community through innovative marketing and events initiatives, Diversity and Inclusion strategies, and corporate citizenship conferences. As CEO, Josefina is responsible for leading business and marketing campaigns, establishing strategic partnerships, and cultivating community relations within multicultural markets.

Before developing RIYHT, Josefina was Founder, Publisher & President of Color Magazine, a Diversity and Inclusion events and publication, focused on creating community, designing leadership conferences, and highlighting the accomplishments of the growing number of professionals of color in the United States. In 2016, Josefina negotiated the successful public sale of Color Magazine to GateHouse Media, one of the largest publishers of locally-based print and online media in the US.

Josefina is an honored and active board member of Eastern Bank, The Museum of Fine Arts, Boston, and The Boys and Girls Club of Massachusetts. She and her two sons currently reside in Boston and spend time at their second home in Puerto Rico. Josefina is currently building a mindfulness retreat and boutique hotel called Catalina del Mar in Puerto Rico that caters to women at the precipice of their careers and lives.

Made in the USA
Middletown, DE
15 December 2019